7 Traits for V.I.C.T.O.R.Y

Expanded Edition

7

Traits for V.I.C.T.O.R.Y

Lessons to power your dreams however high you are
imagining

Sophia L. Burrell

ISBN 978-1517321109

To my two girls, Ariel & Sada, whom I adore.

To all who seek victory

Contents

_____ABOUT THE AUTHOR_____

I must have been one of a few in Jamaica who had three jobs. I worked at the University of the West Indies, Mondays to Fridays, then I took a three-and-a-half-hour trip to Montego Bay, St. James to work nights at Margueritaville Bar and Grill on Friday, Saturday and Sunday. On my weekends in Montego Bay I would interview successful people from the region and write feature articles about them in the Western Mirror. I never thought for a second this was anything exceptional, but I understood that many are reluctant, based on their lack of drive and persistence to make decided effort. I loved writing, so I sought out opportunities that allowed me to do that, and I didn't want to be free on weekends, so I went into Margueritaville and asked the manager if he could hire me for weekends only.

After my arrival in the USA, it was through all my efforts, failures in business, relationships, and networking with others who are making a difference and wanting to succeed like I did, that I came to realize what it takes to achieve. The way I was in Jamaica, I realize that not many were treading that way. I hear excuses all the time why a person cannot do this or that, but they were just that—excuses. They have what it takes, but don't know how to utilize it to their advantage, so excuses become their ally. I've read many biographies and studied successful people and found some commonalities in the way they do things. I've read all of the inaugural speeches of US Presidents and got a sense of their goals and expectations for the country. Ask me why I did this, I don't know, but I felt a need within me and a strong desire to make something of myself and to adopt some of the qualities I see in people who have done well for themselves.

"7 Traits for Victory" is my second book but this is a revised version of it. Looking back I had an idea of what victory entails for the achievement of mastery in any area of life. I wanted to know and be just that. I am not contending that I have all the answers, none of us does, but if persons can be good observers they can pick things up that can actually be the key to making a difference in their lives. My wish is that the concepts presented here will change your thinking and behavior for the better. So much so that every aspect of your life will also change.

For more information, visit: www.sophiaburrell.com

_____INTRODUCTION_____

I started having a relationship with the word victory after I listened to Joyce Myer's CD "Thinking Your Way out of Bondage." She said that you are to speak victory into your life. I didn't know how to do that, but I formulated a phrase based on that word which reads, "I declare victory in my life." I've been using that as a daily incantation for years. There is power in a declaration. I get energized and I would recommend it to anyone who seeks guidance from infinite intelligence.

This book classifies seven traits necessary for victory. Victory is synonymous with mastery, success, conquest and triumph. In this book it's used as an acronym symbolizing the traits essential to success. If you possess these traits, there's a leader in you, and you have what it takes to succeed. All great leaders share similar traits in common, although they might be from a different time, another country, different upbringing, and different levels of education. They are all tenacious, confident, result-oriented, and self-motivated. They possess an optimistic flair in their approach to achievement, and they are leaders who take the initiative to get the results they want.

If there is an art of thinking big, then it has to do with setting big goals. The characteristic traits in this book can be used to power your dreams however high you are imagining. Many people don't have the guts to set lofty goals because they lack some of these traits. You can use this book and its principles to guide you into mastery and the conquest of any goal. You can master these qualities one day at a time by developing the courage to never give up on what you truly aspire to be.

The ringleader among all these traits is confidence. Very few things are achieved or pursued without it. Whatever your endeavor, it requires confidence. You should use this book as a guideline to the way you are supposed to be in your attitude, your thinking, your doing, and your speaking. Whether you just left high school, you are in college, or you've been in the professional arena, these qualities are needed. These qualities are not just for a certain time, they are for all time. They are not just for a selected few, but for anyone with a goal-directed mentality.

History's best are discussed throughout this book. It's important to understand that even men like Julius Caesar could not have been triumphant without these qualities. It was these characteristics that propelled some of them to godlike status. Truly, every one of us has it in us to achieve great things, but for some reason many assume success is for other people.

Persistence is commonly used in everyday language, but I don't believe many realize its actual power. That's where tenacity comes from. The hurdles, obstacles, or challenges one faces on a daily basis cannot be overcome if they surrender to defeat. When you surrender to failure you have basically decided not to persist any longer. Some people simply cannot take the hits in life. Think of all the obstacles that Martin Luther King, Jr. faced, but he persisted. Look at Steve Jobs, everything wasn't always easy breezy for him, but he didn't quit did he? Barack Obama has faced challenges in his life, but obviously that did not stop him from running for, and becoming, President.

I wrote this book based on my experience running my own business and having to cultivate the qualities herein.

Being a business owner, motivational speaker, and immigrant was a tall order I didn't expect. The stories featured in this book should make you more cognizant of the fact that to achieve great success, leaders have to stretch themselves by increasing the size of their goals. It is when your goals appear impossible that you rise up to catch it.

The lessons learned from the tenacity of Thomas Edison, the innovative drive of Bill Gates, the big-thinking ideas of Donald Trump and the inspirational dream of Martin Luther King, Jr. can be used for personal growth. "Success leaves clues," said Jim Rohn. These clues still require certain characteristics for it to manifest. Many don't know how to use the clues so they end up doing nothing. If you learned that Thomas Edison failed more than 6,000 times trying to create the light bulb, that's a clue that indicates that you have to persist and persist until you get it right. If you learned that Michael Jordan, Tiger Woods, and many other sports legends practiced for hours and hours and never stopped trying to improve -- that is a clue.

"Some Traits are like warriors, it fuels your fire, it makes you ruthless, it gives you courage to persist and provide the driving force that yields victory."

- Sophia Burrell

_____Chapter 1_____

VIVACIOUS

VICTORY

Thunder is good, thunder is impressive,

but it's the lightning that does all the work

- Mark Twain

Excitement is contagious, enthusiasm even more so. There is a spark that is illuminated when you are enthusiastic. This spark creates energy, power, life, love, laughter, warmth, or influence—all essential elements to attract success. This is called the vivacious spark (VS). There is no leader, warrior, or goal-oriented person who is not enthusiastic, irrepressible, energetic, active, high-spirited, and positive about winning and achieving. All positive attributes with affective influence on decision-making, action, behavior, and personality. These components represent the precise emotional characteristics you need when talking about your goals, pitching your goals, thinking about your goals or even dreaming about your goals. Bold enthusiasm has character. It draws energy. It's impassioned inclination towards endeavors which people wish to engage or invest in. Enthusiasm has a motivational lineage that influences effort and time spent pursuing a goal. If your goals don't bring you joy, you won't be enthusiastic in your delivery of it. A goal-oriented mentality has high energy, it's engaging, focused and positive. Enthusiasm affects cognition because it refers to a psychological state that activates positive arousal and serves as a barometer that reflects changes in interest or keenness towards a goal. It stimulates the senses garnering more energy and a more positive problem-solving outlook.

If you are excited about what your goals will bring to your life, how it will help other people, and the difference it will make in your world and the outside world, then you can't help but be enthusiastic about it. Enthusiasm is similar to desire and passion (chapter 7), and you are that way because something about your goal resonates with you, like finally realizing what your purpose is.

The opposite of being vivacious is dull, boring, unhappy, inactive, and pessimistic, and you cannot achieve your goals with that mentality. You don't have to change your personality to be vivacious, you just need to bring more energy to your life and endeavors. The dull and boring will suck the life out of a conversation, a party, or a relationship. In reality what they are doing is dimming their own light or dimming the image of their true self. Being vivacious makes you interesting and fun to be around. The next time you enter a room make sure you bring something to it, whether it's laughter, fun, or enthusiasm; be upbeat.

When I first started in business, I was afraid to show my ambitious side. I felt intimidated by my own bold attempt. I felt unqualified, and I questioned myself every day. I was afraid to toot my horn. In retrospect it was gutsy to do what I did, but I felt like a fraud the entire time. I was still new in the country, and that made me feel like I was moving too fast. It's like it was a secret that I started a business. Now I understand why the business didn't work out. The laws of attraction were not on my side because I wasn't even on my side. Those negative emotions drained my energy, and I lost some of the gusto I started with.

If however, I was sharing my goals with the world, feeling confident and excited about a favorable outcome, I might have resonated with people who got the message. I find that when you are bold and enthusiastic about your contributions and the possibility of a favorable outcome, it sends off a different kind of energy that people are attracted to. I should have focused on the positives, and I didn't, because I couldn't see past the things that were riding against me.

Cheering Yourself on:

Do you know that you can cheer yourself on like you do for a winning team? You can. Cheering yourself on means that you stay the course of whatever you are trying to achieve. It means not being afraid to tell the world what you do, because you're proud of it. Tooting your own horn is part of the cheering yourself on process. Cheering yourself on also has to do with believing your time will come. Remember the road is not for the swift but for those who persist. When you internalize and know that you are on to something here, you start to think, "so why quit now?" and you continue to say "yes I can" the world will start to believe you, because you believed.

Per-Assistants, Inc was born after I got laid off from Memorial Sloan Kettering Cancer Center (MSKCC). It was something of a bold experimentation with a focus on providing personal assistants to busy professionals and companies. I am always fascinated by what personal assistants do. They are like trusted allies to many celebrities, CEOs and other professionals. I wanted my personal assistants to have business etiquette training and empowerment sessions to make them well rounded. Not just give them a computer assessment test, like most staffing agency do. I was thinking outside the box without even realizing it. I did some research and found that staffing agencies didn't provide the training that I was offering. It could have worked out is all I am saying, had I been more confident, had I networked more; had I been more persistent. I was too busy being self-conscious and afraid. Any excitement I had was locked up inside, so the law of attraction couldn't find any spark to light a fire.

The biggest lesson from that failure was that I understand now it was just a test to help me become even more tenacious and results-oriented. It was difficult for me at first to come to grips with the fact that I let go because I allowed a lack of confidence todim the view of my outcome expectations which affected my self-judgment. An enthusiastic ideal is a not joke. It's real and powerful. Tooting your horn is about being confident in what you are trying to bring to the table. When you are confident you speak up more and you are not afraid to show your ambitious side. When you are enthusiastic the world becomes curious. If you are self-conscious, or you feel unhappy about your life's choices, you tend to be timid and perhaps afraid to show your ambitious side. When you are vivacious, however, you are basically telling the world you are not afraid. You are telling the world you are irrepressible. Vivaciousness rallies around confidence. It provides nourishment.

Have you ever met a successful person who is not passionate and excited about their goals? Tony Robbins is a great example of someone who is vivacious in spirit. He is like an energy source. Frankly, I've never met the man, but I've seen many interviews with him and listened to all his CDs. Read a couple of his books too. I saw him live at a wealth expo at the Javits Center some years ago.

I was so far at the back that Tony looked like a tiny image in front of me. Whenever he speaks I feel like I want to be part of whatever he's doing. I listen to him and wish I was that smart. I want to do what he does. I want to say what he said. I want to influence people the same way he has done it.

Another thing about being vivacious is that it makes you memorable. Nobody remembers the dull and boring. Go to any network meeting, seminar, and speaker conference and see whom you remember afterwards. When you are excited about your goals, people want to be part of it. They are curious as if something is going on. They think they will miss out on something if they don't join you, or do business with you. That's the power of energy.

Vivacious Spark (VS)

Be careful of the company you keep. Some people will suck the life and light out of you. The people who are in your immediate circle could be responsible for your rise or fall. Do they encourage you? Do they make you feel good about yourself? Do they recognize your talent and congratulate you when you make progress? Do they allow you to stretch? Don't be surprised if your goals suddenly feel like it's not worth it anymore or your passion starts dwindling.

These are some of the reasons why many people don't have victory because their support system keeps chipping away at the value of their dreams, passion, or plans. You can be responsible for the spark that enters a room. Vivacious spark stems from your energy level, which is reflective of what you are doing, saying, and thinking. If you are sad, depressed, or negative, there is no way you're going to carry the vivacious spark around with you.

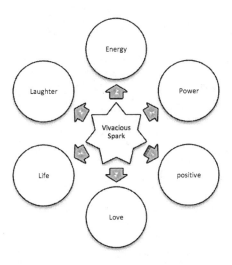

Figure 1. Vivacious Spark

The Mind's Eye

The vivacious spark is in most leaders. Bill Clinton is often described as charismatic. Everybody wants to be his friend. You can see that he enjoys the attention too. He doesn't shy away from people wanting to talk to him or ask him questions. That kind of energy keeps you in the mind of the people who matter. Do you think you could be enthusiastic before you ever set sight on your goals? When Usain Bolt became the fastest man in the world, the world was cheering for him, but did you see his attitude when he crossed the finish line? Can you imagine practicing that before it happened and then to see that it does? Do you think he saw all those wins in his mind before the race? I'm guessing that he practiced that excited win in his mind first. Isn't that what our goals are supposed to do for us? A goal is supposed to fill us with excitement long before we achieve it. We are supposed to feel charged up and ready to go. Your excitement should be about what you intend to accomplish at the end of the journey. Whatever victory is for you; be it money, making people happy, living an extravagant lifestyle, or achieving something so monumental not even you can believe it, it should excite you enough to challenge your status quo.

"Everything you want is outside your comfort zone," said Robert Allen. Here's a question for you. What is it about your dreams that excites you? Are your expected results something to dance about? Even if it is still in the infancy phase, aren't you excited that you had the guts to start. Ben Franklin said, "One today is worth two tomorrows." Why wait to get going.

Key Vivacious Lessons:

- Find a goal that has a resounding effect on you and gives you juice to never stop trying through good and bad times.
- "The Secret" says that energy flows where attention goes. Wherever attention is generated, power follows.

Personal Vivacious Moment:

After I made the decision to become a youth speaker I sent letters out to about 100 high schools in the New York City area, explaining my interest in motivating and empowering their students. I remember telling them that I am on a mission to speak in every high school in New York. I was so pumped and excited about that decision and couldn't wait to get the ball rolling. The enthusiasm I feel about motivating others is totally different from what I felt in my first and second business. What also fueled my excitement was realizing I am good at it, and that I am actually touching students' lives with my message, perhaps changing their perspective on life, shortening their learning curve, giving them a new reality check. When you are motivated you feel more confident to take on bigger and bigger challenges.

Why Do People fail to be Vivacious?

People are afraid to look silly, so they subdue their intensity and bottle up their energy as if there is going to be a strike. The only way to express yourself is with bold enthusiasm. No one wants to be around someone who's dull and boring all the time. Remember that song by Labrinth, "whatever you do, do it good, express yourself, it's not what you look like when you're doing what you do, express yourself." Express yourself!

Vivacious Strategies:

- Because enthusiasm shows the level of influence of a person's goals, it's imperative, therefore, to choose goals that resonate with you. This inevitably affects the value you place on the goal and how much time you choose to spend trying to achieve it.

- Create a music list of songs that make you want to dance (I love oldies and so James Brown's song, "I Feel Good" uplifts my spirit instantly. Also "Little Less Conversation" by Elvis).

- Exercise builds energy. So do more of it. Make a conscious, deliberate effort that you are going to bring your A game every time.

- Remember vivaciousness is about being energetic, and excited and there is nothing negative in those words. Being lively makes you positive, makes you feel good and the people around you will want some of that.

_____Chapter 2_____

INITIATIVE

VICTORY

"Twenty years from now you will be more disappointed by the things that you didn't do than by the ones you did do. So throw off the bowlines. Sail away from the safe harbor. Catch the sail wind in your sails. Explore. Dream. Discover."

– Mark Twain

TO initiate action requires gumption, a kind of predisposition that allows for ingenuity, resourcefulness, originality, and creativity. It is one of the most important qualities of a leader that signifies he/she is not afraid to take proactive steps, adapt to changing environments, be self-motivated, and driven. Having a proactive orientation sets you apart, opens doors, makes you bold, and anything that's bold draws attention, it doesn't fade.

Every runner must take a first step in every race. Every basketball player has to take a step to get on the court. Every golfer has to position himself to take the first swing. Every baby has to take the first step to learn how to walk. There is nothing that started in the middle or at the end. There is a start to everything. There is no winning without a beginning. Although that is true, many are still afraid. Many feel stuck not realizing that the very thing that could set their spirits free is what they've been avoiding.

The Beginning

The willingness or readiness to adapt to the changing environment influences initiative greatly. Nevertheless, everything that surrounds us, everything that we utilize, everything we enjoy and everything we know had a proactive niche. A great example of a beginning is your very inception, and everyone you meet started under those circumstances. That moment when biology takes over and development begins. As old as the earth or the universe itself, there was a beginning. Might be hard to fathom, but even the tallest mountains in the world did not begin at that level, but they started somewhere. When something is finished being built, it's hard to remember where it all began, but everything on this planet started somewhere, no matter how miniscule its creation or inexplicable its inception.

Christopher Columbus discovered vast lands. He had the courage to put Spain behind him so he could discover what was beyond the horizon. He certainly wouldn't have discovered new lands if he hadn't taken the initiative that started the course of his legendary journey. He wouldn't be the man I am writing about today. He would not be in the history books or be the personality that every single high school discusses in history class. We all learn history in high school and, although I grew up in Jamaica, I was still taught about Columbus' voyages. In fact, on his third trip from Spain he had to dock in St. Anne's Bay, Jamaica, because one of the ship's bottoms had rotted out. It was much like an emergency landing. He and his crew were marooned in Jamaica for about a year before help arrived. His bold expedition created the Spanish colonization which wouldn't have taken place had he been afraid. Columbus' arrival changed history.

He had to borrow money for his voyages across the Atlantic, and he was surrounded by people who did not believe in his quest. King John II of Portugal was one of them. Columbus twice asked him for funding to explore the West (the Atlantic Ocean) and was denied both times. In fact, King John II stole his idea and sent a crew for this voyage only to find trouble out at sea and have to return. There is proof that Columbus was a determined businessman because, after his second attempt at asking King John II for help failed, he went to the Spanish Courts, and it was there that Queen Isabella approved his trip. In fact, she approved all four trips he made across the Atlantic. Approval for these trips did not come easily. Columbus had to wait eight years. And even after he got approval, he was only given three small ships for his voyage. The Pinta, the Santa Maria, and the Nina were all about eighty feet long, smaller than regular ships of that day.

The Meaning of Initiative:

Self-motivation is the best definition I could find that totally translates to the message of this chapter. Self-motivation runs deep like the ocean. Its appeal is gigantic. It reflects the true meaning of the first chapter because one's own enthusiasm on a particular interest greatly influences initiative, or the ability to adapt to that space. A first move, an introductory act, or eagerness to do something, or a beginning, also address the meaning of the word. This is the part that scares people. That initial act is why many don't pursue their dreams. The first step is the biggest step, and probably carries more meaning or weight. Nothing will be achieved if nobody makes the first move. Every leader knows that it's important to initiate conversations, change a course of action, be resourceful, inventive, and original. The opposite, however, is to remain indifferent or simply inactive. It you remain indifferent you'll never start anything. Indifference carries an unenthusiastic tone which puts out all fires and makes you appear unconcerned. Success in life involves a combination of traits, each providing fuel for the other.

Self-motivation and victory

It goes without saying that in order to achieve at the highest level a proactive orientation is necessary. Self-motivation influences performance, guides effort, and makes you committed despite challenges. Self-motivation guides goal-directed behavior. Notice that a person who is self-motivated has a sense of their perceived self-efficacy and self-beliefs, which often impacts how they face challenges, and how they push themselves to achieve and persist in the face of difficulties.

The Perception of Failure:

Say, for example, you took the initiative and started your own business, but things didn't work out. What do you do then? Would you give up and say at least I tried? Or do you tweak the plans you had, restart with greater fervor, learn from what you did wrong and give it another go? The good thing about mistakes is that you learn some lessons about what not to do the next time. You have to treat setbacks as lessons and not death sentences. Failures are lessons that perhaps your plans weren't as sound. When you were just learning how to ride a bike, how many times did you fall before you got it right? You hurt your knees, perhaps? You got a few scratches. But you tried, and tried, until you got it right.

Your starting point is where decisions are made. It is where you decide that you are going to give it everything you've got. It is where you decide that no matter what, you are going to make it. It is where you decide this girl is worth it, let's get married. It's a starting point to greatness, to success, to what makes you fulfilled and happy. It is before you take the first step that you decide that you are not going to lose a race, a relationship, an exam, a business. From there you step into the possibilities, and it is an endless possibility, because you will find every opportunity to build your dream, to advance, to progress, to move forward and to grow. When you decide to "go for it," your creative juices start finding ways to help you master the journey. Your decision will push every one of the "what ifs" aside. You are now so committed that, no matter how bad things get, you will never give up. Your efforts are now mobilized and ready to go.

Fear is an illusion

Fear is a bully. Fear immobilizes efforts and make many oversensitive, paralyzed, and unhappy. Now, there is no reason, after all we've been through as African Americans, and what we have sacrificed to attain some level of progress, that people would still be afraid to move forward and make decisions that would enhance their lives. But that is not the case. Many cannot see the light at the end of the tunnel. Many are still holding back and are afraid to succeed. I had a conversation with a friend recently; he is in his late 50s but he cannot seem to move his mind past the 1990s. He is always talking about what whites did to blacks, and that it's a white man's country. He lives in the past, and he cannot get out. He is afraid to start a business. He is afraid to put his money in the bank, he's afraid to try, even afraid to be positive. He lives in a constant state of "what if." He is simply afraid. Although he speaks intelligently and is fairly educated, he is always of the assumption that government is after him or something. He is paranoid and his paranoia has prevented any real progress in his life. Any conversation with him and optimism and confidence quickly disappear.

Developing a proactive orientation is not hard, although it requires courage. It depends on what you are taking the step towards. Taking the first step towards something that you cannot yet see whether it will be favorable or not might be hard, but that's what taking risk and chances are all about. Being proactive sounds risky to many, and perhaps, to a certain degree, it is, but life itself is a risk. Starting a relationship is risky, getting married is risky, driving on the freeway is risky, and childbirth is risky. Anything one starts is risky because that's life. Playing it safe and being too cautious is not living. You're not going to be the only one who will never leave earth alive so why be afraid to do something that could possibly enhance your life. "You miss 100% of the chances you never take," said Michael Jordan. Remember Columbus was not sure what he would discover if he sailed west. Dr. King didn't know he would win a Nobel Peace prize when he took the chance of spearheading the Civil Rights movement. President Obama wasn't sure he would win the primary against a robust Hillary Clinton. Don't forget her husband Bill Clinton is a beloved former President. One might have assumed putting the two odds together that Clinton as a woman would be a more favorable bet than Obama being black.

Chris Matthews of "Hardball" said at the beginning of the campaign that only God could beat Hillary if she runs for president. I suppose God decided not to make that happen. Fear is an illusion but it will snatch your goals away before you even realize it. Be careful, it's a sneaky bastard. If you constantly focus on the obstacles that might show up you will never get anywhere. I am confident that fear is one major reason why many are afraid to do anything worthwhile about their plight. Worrying whether challenges will come knocking can discourage anybody. But these are not solutions they are dream stealers. This is where confidence comes in and regulating each step you have to take.

Key Lessons from Christopher Columbus?

- His desire to sail west was denied twice by a greater authority. But that didn't stop him from asking someone else for help. Apart from taking the initiative to ask someone else he was adamant and persistent in getting what he wanted to make that trip possible. So began the journey of discovering new lands across the Atlantic. His initiative led to some great discoveries.

- Columbus' action was that of a leader. The answer "no" was not an answer for him, it was motivation. Leaders don't fold. They take action. It was clear that Columbus was not waiting around for someone to tell him what to do. He had a burning desire. He had to get the funds to sail west. He simply had to.

- Columbus was at sea for a good six weeks with no sight of land. If you were in his shoes, would you have turned back? Remember he didn't know what he would find. He took a chance.

- He had the ability to come up with an original concept and discovered many undiscovered lands.

Personal Moment on Initiative:

I have never been afraid of taking risks, so taking the initiative was never an issue for me. I remember clearly, though, when I decided that, instead of going back to work, I would instead start my own business. I worked in a lab at Memorial Sloan Kettering Cancer Center (MSKCC); they shut everything down and moved to Columbia University. I am grateful they let me go. Otherwise I wouldn't have started my own business. I wouldn't have written two books. I wouldn't be speaking at graduation ceremonies and be empowering high school students and employees.

The idea that I don't have to answer to anybody but myself was very enticing. So I set everything in motion; got my license, bonded, and incorporated my business, and launched a website. I was officially in business. There were a lot of things to do in the initial phase which took me off guard. I see why starting a business might be intimidating, but when you get the basic foundation stuff out of the way, the real work begins - trying to find clients. I did some research and learned about what I needed to move forward and where to go to get help. Once you've decided to start your own business, you never stop moving and thinking creatively about what to do to make it work. You are constantly trying to find solutions. That's self-motivation at work.

Why Do People Fail to Take the Initiative?

Fear of failure is a big concern for many people and the reason why many lose their drive and motivation to start moving towards accomplishing something meaningful. Initiative requires making a decision and since fear makes decisions for many people, inaction results. The decision to start signifies that the individual might have to adapt to what's new in the space they intend to capture.

I find it amazing that people would rather give up on their dreams than to take a chance at adapting to change. Not realizing that there is no succeeding without exposing yourself to risk. There is no succeeding without overcoming something to get there. If everybody were scared to do everything, we would still be living in darkness, we would still be riding carriages. There would be no airplanes, there would be no women's liberation, slavery would still exist, and blacks would still be an uneducated group of people. Segregation would still be rampant. There would be no Constitution, or even a decision to be independent. The world would be really dull and boring if nobody wanted to start or initiate change for a better life. Usually after one person takes the first step everybody follows. Part of being a leader is not waiting for other people to make the first move. Leadership requires daring, audacity and uncompromising efforts towards and a purpose. You will never get there without self-determined effort.

Strategies for Initiative:

- Adaptability is what you should seek. Learning to adapt to changing environments is a positive predisposition.
- Initiative has close ties to one's self-regulation, which affects all the traits mentioned in this book, particularly optimism and confidence. If one is optimistic about his or her outcome it will influence the actions and responsibility they take in any environment.

- Responsibility means that persons have the ability to control and adapt to the shaping of their own lives by being proactive.

- It is fearing the implications of what might occur when an action is initiated that brings about inaction. Therefore, self - discipline/control/persistence to start a course and see it through is required.

_____Chapter 3_____

CONFIDENCE

VI**C**TORY

Believe in yourself and there will come a day when others

will have no choice but to believe with you

– Cynthia Kersey

I CAN say with certainty that no one feels confident or self-assured 100 percent of the time. Yet nothing significant is ever achieved without it. Self-confidence and self-esteem are intimately linked. There's a causal effect of confidence on a person's orientation, be it goal-orientation, proactive orientation, motivation, and action. It is a proximal element that affects everything we do. But confidence in essence is faith. If you have faith in the abilities you have to achieve the goals you've set for yourself, nothing can deter you from making it a reality.

You don't need knowledge and money to be confident, although knowledge is an important factor. Having confidence means you have esteem for yourself and you value yourself enough to set your goals high towards self-actualization. The self-confidence factor is critical to any achievement outcome. But is confidence a reflection of our self-concept? People who are confident walk taller. Their eyes smile. There is something different in their attitude and in their walk. They look you in the eye when they talk to you because they believe firmly in who they are. The confident trait is very attractive. It's like fragrance that uplifts the air. When you smell something pleasant it yields positive emotion and that's what confidence does.

Confidence is at the center of attention and all the other traits feed from it. Imagine being part of a circle and there is a leader in the middle of that circle. The leader is confidence. Without confidence many goals don't see the light of day. Many dreams are not realized, because people lack emotional intelligence to trust themselves and to properly monitor their self-talk and their self-judgment.

Confidence relays instructions to self-efficacy, self-concept, self-motivation, and self-esteem. Its characteristics are positively related to the seven traits written about in this book. There is no way to achieve anything worthwhile without being confident. Confidence is part of every success equation. It is a quality that affects every idea, journey, performance, action and behavior.

Having success and confidence doesn't mean you have no inadequacies. Every successful person has scars. Perhaps not a physical scar but something they're mindful of. You would probably be surprised to learn what many successful people have been through, although they appear confident. But that's the magic of confidence! You can gain confidence after you've overcome the biggest trial in your life, because you didn't allow it to undermine your self-worth. It's a great strength finder when you learn how to triumph over difficulties. The thing is, many people, whether adults or teens, men or women, focus on their weaknesses instead of focusing on what is great about themselves. Dwelling on your inadequacies all the time does not build confidence.

Figure 2. Confidence is Key

Mohammed Ali:

There is no denying that Mohammed Ali is a cultural icon. He is Sportsman of the century, athlete of the century, sports personality of the century and world's sportsman of the century. Out of all the great athletes in the world, it was Ali that they chose for those titles. Ali was a professional boxer but you'd be convinced he's a professional optimist. You cannot talk about Ali without talking about his confident view of life, his famous quotes and his famous fights.

The reason why he is so iconic is that there is so much more to him and about him than what he was as a boxer. When a man says, "I am going to show you how great I am," you better believe him. When he said he wrestled with an alligator and tussled with a whale, I believed him. Didn't you? When he said he'd handcuff lightning and throw thunder in jail, I didn't doubt him for a minute. His words, "I am the greatest" became a self-fulfilling prophesy and no doubt was what led him to fight and try even harder.

Finding your Confidence

Ali knew he was a great boxer. It takes a tough talent to be the heavyweight champion three times. You can gain confidence by realizing your talent and your abilities. What is it that you are complimented on regularly? What can you brag about like Ali did, because you are that good at it? What comes easy to you? Confidence comes from the inside out. It's emotional intelligence, self-trust, self-belief, attitude, the ability to do something efficiently, execution, prowess and intuitiveness. It's an inner feeling of assurance knowing who you are, what you want, and liking yourself in the process.

Finding your confidence boils down to knowing what you are good at and accepting yourself for who you are. The intuitive part of confidence doesn't always come as a well-practiced skill. You might not have all the information you need in a particular area but confidence brings out your intuitive side and makes you believe, and most important, take action.

Before you go any further in this book, pause here and answer the questions in the table below. Be honest with yourself. Gauge your traits on a scale of 1 - 10. How confident are you? When you look in the mirror what is it that you like most? Do you believe that as beautiful as Angelina Jolie is, she's not mindful of something about her body? What is it about you that overrides all the faults you always find? That should be your focus. Were there not for these faults, mistakes, or challenges, would you be more confident? Know this, successful people have some of the same challenges, but they use their subjective convictions and still move on, still smile, still try, still build on what they've lost, despite criticism or ridicule.

What comes easy to you?	What are you complimented on regularly?	What can you brag about like Ali did because you're good at it?

Figure 3. Finding your Strength

Identify your strength with this exercise table and use what you discover. From now on, never allow the small thinking part of you to convince you that you are not good enough, or that you cannot have victory. Doubt your own doubts and insecurities. Trust yourself. Test your resolve. Pay particular or deliberate attention to the actions you take as well as your internal narrative. Use self-judgment to structure and weigh your personal standards. Psychological vulnerabilities are established through low confidence and low self-esteem. You want to be mindful of that.

Confidence can be recognized everywhere. Anyone who goes after their goal despite challenges or screw-ups must have the confident trait within them. So it's fair to say that if a person wants something and is not going after it, they lack confidence. Any technology you use today, anything that makes you comfortable, even the clothes you wear, your haircut or color, the food you eat, the books you've read that inspired you, the classes you took—were created by someone who had the belief that it could be done and they made it happen. When you are confident you take action. It's that's simple. It is people who lack confidence who go to their graves with their dreams still unrealized because it was all in their heads and they never did anything about it. It is people who lack confidence who sit in their rocking chairs when they get old and regret that they never tried. The less confident you are, the less action you take.

Less Confidence, less action

Sticking to your goals until you win or until it yields is not rocket science. One major problem for lack of success in many people is that they lack the confidence to make the effort necessary for the realization of their dream. They don't have the confidence to think big, and so they settle for mediocrity. Thinking big relates to confidence. Many people are reluctant to admit that the reason they feel so comfortable in their comfort zone is because they lack the confidence, commitment, and the courage that a challenge requires. With goals comes certain expectations, habits, values, and needs. When these factors are not fully realized, individuals will quickly compare themselves to others as if it's impossible for them to achieve the same. The bottom line is they are insecure, full of self-doubt, and probably have low self-esteem.

Life is not a three strikes and you are out kind of thing. If you want something badly enough, go get it, and stick with it until it yields. Life is about moving from failure to failure until you succeed. If you give up in the process, perhaps your expectations weren't high enough, and you didn't value your goals like you claim you did. The equation of life looks a lot like this: Life = failure + success $(L = f + S)$.

If you add failure to success it will still be success. If you minus failure from success it is failure. There is no success without failing first. There is no success without overcoming some kind of odds. Confidence is about realizing what is stacked against you, but never letting it stop you. It is a learning process from whichever angle you choose to look. If you are looking for an easy way out, there is no easy way out. Joyce Myers said, the only way out is through.

In Napoleon Hill's book "Think and Grow Rich" is a poem that builds confidence.

> If you think you are beaten, you are
>
> If you think you dare not, you don't
>
> If you like to win, but you think you can't
>
> It is almost certain you won't ......

In practicing self-confidence you have to exercise some level of control over your self-talk and thoughts and be critical. There is an art to thinking that can maximize your efforts, alleviate self-doubt and repudiate negative influences. The power of confidence has been the subject of interest perhaps before the famous words of Julius Caesar "men willingly believe what they wish." This is still applicable today. People wish to think they cannot achieve certain goals or they choose to think they can.

Perhaps as well, you can use another quote from Caesar and conquer your fears. He said, "I came, I saw and I conquered." To conquer something means that you overcome it by force, or you win by great effort. Isn't that what you are supposed to do for your goals anyway? Conquering the obstacles that stands between you and your goals is winning the battle and fighting a good fight to get to where you are supposed to be.

There's a boldness and defiance that always travels with confidence and the life of Julius Caesar was a perfect depiction of that. He was a ruthless warrior with only winning on his mind. Caesar's conquest of Gaul was nothing short of a bold expedition. He wanted the whole of France and Belgium to be a Roman province. Imagine setting a goal so big it seems near impossible to achieve. There is one word that was always used to describe Caesar and that is ambitious. He had an earnest desire for achievement, power, distinction and wealth. His campaign to get what he wanted was very ambitious to say the least. After campaigning and fighting for six years Gaul was finally won. Caesar became dictator of Rome.

Gaul was made up of multitude of states called Celts. These Celts housed many hostile tribes that were far from unified. He was able to defeat them one tribe at a time. The German tribes particularly were barbaric and uncivilized and threatened Caesar's goal for Rome. They were basically trying to expand in the Rhine and Caesar wouldn't have it. If he hadn't defeated them, they would certainly have taken over Rome. Much like your fears, if you don't conquer it, it will conquer you.

He was increasingly uneasy after the conquest of Gaul because he thought there was nobody around him he could trust except Cicero. Plus he didn't have a son to be the next heir, so he adopted his nephew Augustus (Octavian). This might have been one of the best decisions Caesar made because after his assignation Augustus was immediately thrust into the treacherous waters of politics where he ruled for 49 years. He also became the first Emperor of Rome during this time. He is known as one of Rome's greatest rulers. His reign created a dynasty that lasted close to a century.

Key Lessons about confidence from Julius Caesar?

- You have to be bold and defiant to get what you want. Without that ruthless warrior attitude Caesar would have been unable to achieve his goal.

- Caesar was gutsy, confident, and full of himself which were the perfect ingredients to battle his way through.

- The battle was long and hard, but he never lost sight of his end goal, which was to win Gaul and rule Rome. Remember, it took him six long years to win Gaul.

- Confidence is more than a feeling. It's that thing in your gut that leads you and guides you. Reason and wise caution cannot restrain confidence.

Key Lessons about confidence from Mohammed Ali?

- Ali's confidence was impressive both in and out of the ring. When he declared he was the greatest, you think he didn't believe it? He knew he was. Find a fuel-filled affirmation that can light your fire every time you say it.

- Ali said he had to do something different for his next fight and wrestling with an alligator and tussling with a whale was his strategy. What are you going to do different to guarantee that you will win your personal battles? To have a chance at actually achieving your goals, what strategy will you use?

Personal Confident Moment:

I remember when I first started speaking in high schools, I had a message I wanted to speak about, but I was unsure how it would be received. I was nervous but I learned from those experiences that you just push on through. I had to have faith in myself that I could deliver, and the icebreaker that I developed always helped smooth the presentation over. When students start laughing, it's a great place to start teaching. When they laugh it opens the door for the learning to begin. My icebreaker is a confidence booster thanks to Mohammed Ali. I always asked for three or four volunteers and when they come up to join me I asked each of them to repeat, "I am going to show you how great I am." They are to say it with an attitude like they are bragging that they are great. It always cracks up the entire class or auditorium when the volunteers try to say those famous words. When people enjoy what you've created it has a tendency of boosting your confidence.

Why people lack confidence?

People lack confidence because they are filled with self-doubt due to some imperfect knowledge about themselves. There's an interaction between a person's perceived self-efficacy, personal effort, and self-confidence. Imagine, therefore, having negative influences attached to all of these components. Lack of confidence dulls motivation which reduces individual drive towards a goal, and is a determining factor in how high or low goals are set. Effort exerted is reflective on these elements. Self-doubt carves negative thinking patterns in one's cognitive process. If you want to get into public speaking for example, but you think you might suck, you will never start. Believing in yourself even when others don't is natural. When I first got into public speaking I was fearful that my accent would turn people off or I would mess up and people would laugh at me. I had to practice over and over and over again what I wanted to say. In psychology rehearsal is important to conditioning as well as transferring information to long term memory. Plus I would encourage myself along the way with my fuel filled affirmation.

I remember making the decision to be youth speaker. I went to the department of education office and asked them what to do if I wanted to go into schools with the intent to empower and motivate students to be their best selves. It was there that I got the schoolbook of all the high schools that are in the five boroughs of New York City. Nothing was going to stop me from getting it done after I made up my mind that was what I wanted to do. Self-confidence also is about reassuring yourself of what you are capable of, setting certain standards and values for yourself. Action is the best thing you can do to get rid of fear. It mobilizes your creativity. It's all about what you focus on, too. If you focus on all the things that can go wrong you will never do anything. But when you focus on what you hope to gain, your self-confidence will start to improve. Remember you can work on being confident. It's a self-regulative process. You are the one in charge, not fear. Don't allow fear to make your decisions.

Strategies for Building Confidence:

- Accepting yourself for who you are, is an important step in liking yourself, trusting what you want as well as trusting your capabilities.

- Focus on your strengths. Whatever you do best is what you need to focus on. Never underestimate your self-worth. You are as valuable as anybody. Know in your gut that you matter.

- We are all unique which means none of us are inferior to anybody. Use your uniqueness as a plus. Why would you want to be somebody else? Look around you; everybody is different and beautiful in their own way.

- You don't need other people to validate your importance. The fact that you were born is good enough reason.

- If it is an experience or mistake you've made that is preventing you from being confident, know this; there's a cicatrix attached to every living soul, maybe it's not physical but something they are mindful of.

_____Chapter 4_____

TENACITY

VIC**T**ORY

Many of life's failures are people who did not realize how close

they were to success when they gave up

-Thomas Edison

There is no successful person on the planet who doesn't have the tenacity trait flowing in his blood. Tenacity gives you the power to hold on to your dreams with an iron-like grip. Tenacity teaches persistence and resilience. What night is to day is what tenacity is to your goals. If it's one thing high achievers have in common it is this trait.

Passing the tenacity test is more critical than you realize. There is no clear path without challenges, setbacks or obstacles. It is critical to the extent where millions fail due to their inability to see that it's just a test that measures performance, reliability, commitment or quality of your goals. A winner however always manages to overcome based on the lessons learned from this test. Those are the people who always move from failure to failure and never lose steam. They are always inspired by their failures rather than be defeated by them. A tenacious person is not easily discouraged, they don't give up, they never quit. They know very well that the only way to reach their goal is to jump the hurdles and move forward.

Thomas Edison was without question a tenacious legend. He failed 6,000 times trying to create the light bulb. We would probably still be darkness if it weren't for him. I can't imagine 6,000 failures. I had two business failures, and I was devastated. 6,000 is beyond my imagination. Despite my failed business I kept going, though, I never quit. As soon as the sting of failure wears off, I am back again trying something new or fixing what went wrong. Success requires an unyielding tenacity.

Michelangelo

The Sistine Chapel would basically have no character without the paintings of Michelangelo. He is the epitome of tenacity in its truest form. The Sistine Chapel is located in the Vatican where priests are ordained or elected. It is a very sacred part of the chapel. His task was to portray the twelve apostles on the ceiling, and it took him a reported four years 1508 – 1512 to complete. Imagine this for a moment, painting in an awkward position that's causing your back and neck muscles to hurt and then having to bend backwards in order to paint above and behind your head. Imagine also painting an entire area only to find out that mold has taken over the area due to the damp weather. This made it near impossible for the plaster to cure, so he had to restart. Know that this was four years of labor across 5,000 square feet of frescoes. In addition to that, the Pope was frequently ill (and near death) and Michelangelo was in jeopardy of not being paid. Michelangelo himself said, "after four tortured years, more than 400 over-life-size figures, I felt as old and as weary as Jeremiah. I was only 37, yet friends did not recognize the old man I had become."

It's funny to think that Michelangelo complained to Pope Julius II that he is a sculptor not a painter, but the Pope insisted that Michelangelo must paint the chapel. If it weren't for the insistence of the Pope, the chapel wouldn't have been painted. Could you ever imagine subjecting yourself in this manner to achieve your goals? The end result is beautiful, isn't it? So why is it that people don't focus on that? That's the beauty about tenacity -- it powers you forward. It's like a drill that carves out creative ways to accomplish your goals. It creates possibilities. It's a titan of a quality to possess. The opposite however, is being fickle, weak, surrendering, and perfidious because you breach that faith and loyalty you should have when trying to reach a goal.

Key Lessons about tenacity from Michelangelo?

- No matter how bad it gets keep moving forward. Years of hard labor can dull the vision of your goals. Be patient.
- Even if you have to start over. Don't let the start over process make you lose focus. During the first year of the task, all the painted portions had to be removed and the entire procedure had to be redone. This was frustrating for sure. Has that ever happened to you? You start a task and realize halfway in that something is wrong and you just have to do it over. Do you know that many people would have quit at this point? I am reminded of what happened to Joyce Myers when she was

writing one of her books. She said she had written a few chapters and lo and behold everything got wiped out from the computer. She didn't know what happened. She talked about it for months because she was so frustrated with herself and realizing also that she just had to start over.

- If you have to bend over backward to reach your goals, it probably won't kill you, it might make you stronger or in the very least more flexible. Without a doubt it takes patience and commitment to achieve what Michelangelo did. Painstakingly painting images awkward to his normal body movements. Although the Pope had to force and threaten him to start the Sistine Chapel, his commitment to it was undeniable. His patience is commendable and is a testament to his faith. Genius is eternal patience he said.

- You might discover strength and talent you never knew you had. Tenacity brightens your light and shows who you really are. I wonder if Michelangelo knew he had that kind of talent in him. Why didn't he want to be known as a Painter? Yet it was his skill as a painter that led to his brilliance and success.

- If you stretch yourself, it is the stretching of the mind and body that allows all the creative juices to get the job done. You might even discover a new talent. Michelangelo stretched himself and discovered he's a genius of a painter. He did say, "Every block of stone has a statue inside it and it is the task of the sculptor to discover it." It seemed like he had a love affair with sculpting, because he also said, "I saw an angel in the marble and carved until I set it free."

- People have the tendency to only see when you "arrive" never seeing the hard work that was done. That's why I agree with Michelangelo that if people knew how hard he had to work to gain his mastery, it wouldn't seem wonderful at all.

- It can take you longer than you anticipate to achieve your goals. Some goals are not visible until after years of hard work. Obstacles are always lurking around the corner. It is probably safe to say that if Michelangelo had quit or didn't do the

Sistine Chapel, he wouldn't be part of the Italian renaissance.

- Michelangelo could easily be described as a tenacious legend. The Sistine Chapel might be his most famous work but if you look at his other jobs the same brilliance is evident. He was certainly no flip flapper. His genius was consistent.

- He lived until he was 88 years old, so the arduous task of completing the Sistine chapel and his other jobs certainly did not kill him. Many people have the attitude that if they take another step forward into a task, they won't make it out alive. Obviously, I don't know you personally, but I can bet that your journey to your goals is not as hard as painting the Sistine Chapel.

Personal Tenacious Moment:

After the sting of the end of my first business wore off I jumped right back in to start a second. I am not comfortable being anyone's employee. The second time was a concierge service. In the first business I was providing personal assistants to busy professionals, and the second I was the concierge providing the same services to professionals. A concierge service seemed less complicated, plus, I was the personal assistant running all the errands. "Success consists of going from failure to failure without any loss of enthusiasm," said Winston Churchill. Actually that sounds like the definition of tenacity.

Why People fail to be Tenacious

People lose their drive for many reasons but the biggest obstacle to success is within their own minds. Failures can carve negative thinking patterns which consequently put an end to goals, sometimes life itself. People allow their circumstances, failures, mistakes and criticisms to block the optimistic view of their goals. People allow setbacks to deride their efforts. They will complain all day long about what went wrong instead of finding solutions to fix the problem. And they allow their minds to get stuck in that very place. They allow the mistakes or the setback to define who they are and once that happens, it sucks their energy and destroys any confidence left to go forward.

Remember tenacity is about holding firm to your purpose and remaining steadfast to your goals with unwavering faith. If you are not doing that, then you are not being tenacious.

Tenacity is in Every Success Story:

I have no doubt that if you have a conversation with any successful person you will find that tenacity was their closest ally and explains why they expend so much effort. Take athletes as an example, the more effort they expend over a long period, the more they are able to master a performance. This is also true for any endeavor. Winning is about grasping firmly to your ideals and never giving up. The funny thing is, winners make it appear like their journey was easy, when in fact it was anything but. When you are on the outside looking in, it's difficult to see the hard work. Have you ever heard the saying, "walk a mile in my shoes"? The shoes would never fit, because you might not have the same determination. You would never get up at 3, 4 or 5 a.m to practice for years and years until you master a task. You will not practice throwing a ball in the hoop all day long until you get it right. You will not practice until your feet bleed.

To be triumphant takes guts, determination, gumption and a never give up, I can do this attitude. I can and I am, are powerful words. The next time you feel like giving up, just remember that you have to commit yourself to the goals you are trying to achieve. If you are not committed you won't make it. Part of achieving goals is your commitment to it. The bottom-line is when you persist you are in essence sticking with your commitment. When you obligate yourself to the fulfillment of your dreams, that's tenacity. According to Les Brown, "no matter how bad it gets, I am going to make it."

It was Jim Rohn who said that "success leave clues," and he is absolutely right. Obama will leave a legacy that every black child or man will try to emulate. Michelle Obama, too, is a great role model as the first black first lady. Many upcoming talk show hosts will undoubtedly want to follow in Oprah's footsteps. Steve Jobs has left a legacy that no one will soon forget. Success is everywhere. Tyler Perry is one of the highest paid celebrities in Hollywood and people are flocking to work with him. Many people overlook the tenacious journey of the successful. Even if you are aware of their journey and the steps they took to make it, if you don't have the same persistent nature you probably won't get to the same level. Persistence runs deep, and is a subtle guide to success. There is no succeeding without it.

Strategies for becoming Tenacious/Passing the Test

- Tenacity requires calculated discipline to stay on a course that turned out to be bumpy
- Hurdle your obstacles and keep moving forward
- Tenacity is a form of commitment. It makes you hold on for better or worse. Nothing affects goals more astringently than commitment.
- Goal-directed behavior requires regulating the conditions that affect one's life.
- When you establish a standard of which to attain your goals, stick with it.

_____Chapter 5_____

OPTIMISM

VICT**O**RY

A pessimist sees the difficulty in every opportunity;

an optimist sees the opportunity in every difficulty

- Winston Churchill

Martin Luther King, Jr. was without question a warrior for the Civil Rights movement. Not warrior in the classical sense, but someone who stood up when leadership in the black community was lacking. Every black man, woman, and child were scared during that time of civil unrest. For him to step forward and be our voice was tremendously brave. Being optimistic is important. Anticipating a favorable outcome affects behavior and a person's approach to life. How problems are accosted, how misfortune and difficulties are handled, have impacting attributes. An inverse effect would have led to hopelessness.

His belief that blacks would ultimately triumph was ambitious to say the least. Optimism and resilience during affliction is the highest long-term predictor of success. Optimism and confidence are intimately linked; the same is true for pessimism and doubts. Both either positive or negative provide some rationale for an outcome. For him to be hopeful for a successful outcome for blacks seemed far-fetched at the time. But it was obvious his optimism was charged up when he said, "in spite of the difficulties and frustrations of the moment, I still have a dream." The importance of a goal increases it value. It is obvious now what his efforts accomplished. Many would agree that we are still lagging behind in many areas, but we cannot deny the strides we have taken. Who knows what course our paths would have taken if MLK did not instill that dream in the black community. He died too soon, as I am sure there was so much more left in him.

Many falter on the optimistic scale due to their interpretation of past events. What's past is what they use to predict future outcomes, that is, they use no formal calculations, only personal judgments/opinions. Failure is inevitable or will remain when people assume it's a firmly-established way of life. Pessimism rarely leads to favorable outcomes because it's a kind of negative pattern that promotes the development of cognitive distortion which ultimately causes a disengagement from any attempt to apply one's self. As you know, without effort most goals are lost and motivation wanes.

History might have been very different, if in his mind's eye, Dr. King did not see blacks living equally and having the same opportunities. Perhaps there wouldn't be a Civil Rights movement, which started because of his beliefs. He wouldn't have taken a stand. According to the Seattle Times blacks have gained economic ground since the height of the Civil Rights movement, and it was in honor of MLK's legacy that the government established his birthday as a national holiday.

Looking back at all the brave souls, Rosa Parks being one them, who were not afraid to initiate the fight against discrimination and the fight to initiate change, one has to wonder what would have happened if our heroes hadn't had an optimistic view of our future. When MLK learned about Rosa Parks' bold resistance, he organized the Boycott of the Montgomery Buses. And although it took them a year before the Supreme Court intervened and called the segregation of the buses unconstitutional, for one lady to defy authority like that, what an initiation for change that was. What a confident move she made. She was a pioneer for change. They make living today easier and more meaningful.

History is not without people who made change happen by their willingness to act, start the conversation, begin retaliation, and push progress. In the 48 Laws of Power it said that, "audacity separates you from the herd. Boldness gives you presence, and makes you seem larger than life." Rosa's bold interpretation of not getting up to give a white person her seat obliterated some of the gaps that stood between whites and blacks at the time. Although she was arrested, there is no comparison between that and the impact of her actions. Martin Luther King was rewarded when he became the youngest recipient of the Nobel Peace Prize. This prize was attributed to his leadership of the non-violent resistance to racial prejudice.

Key Lessons about optimism from Martin Luther King and Rosa Parks?

- Being optimistic that there will be change during affliction and resistance is very hard. Nevertheless it has been done, so it can be done.

- Although the beginning of a thing might be the most dreadful, you won't move forward if you don't try. MLK said you don't have to see the whole staircase, just take the first step. This signifies the importance of faith and faith takes courage. It takes courage to subject one's self to a cause that's unpopular.

- Challenging racism in America was a big step, and men like MLK were brave enough to initiate the fight which led to progress. MLK lived in a time when he should have been scared to publicly retaliate against the whites for discriminating against the blacks.

- He took the initiative, nevertheless, to lead the black community, which basically placed him front and center in the line of fire. Blacks, although inspired by his dreams, are still weary of the word "equality" since instances of discrimination and prejudice continue to loom.

- Rosa Parks said she was defiant that day because she realized that "….the more we gave in, the more we complied with that kind of treatment, the more oppressive it became."
- Stand up for the things you believe in.

Personal Optimistic Moment:

I always try to visualize a favorable outcome, which is hard when times are tough. It's imperative to have an optimistic view on whatever you are about to embark. It's sometimes nerve wracking when I have to speak in front of a large crowd. But I would imagine people laughing and having a good time. Because I believe that my message is indeed life changing and many people are being empowered to the point where they actually develop better thinking habits which move them to take action in some way shape or form, I'm happy with that.

Why People fail to remain optimistic:

It's hard to be optimistic when everything is going wrong, right? It's hard to see the bright side of the darkness.

Nevertheless, it is paramount for success. To keep your sanity, optimism is imperative. A person cannot succeed being negative all the time. Achieving one's goal is a positive emotion; not carrying that emotion with you before it is realized can be a detriment to the journey.

There are times when optimism does not come easy, it has to be forced. You have to force yourself to eliminate negativism. Optimism takes practice. Have you ever been around someone who tells you they are not a pessimist, but all that comes out of his or her mouth are negative connotations? Pessimists are the worst kind to be around, and because they've lived in that mindset for so long they have no clue, that's who they are. They never see the silver living around a dark cloud. If things are going downhill, they will say, "see I told you." Optimism, although it's a stable trait, can be mustered. You have to think it, speak it, and then do it.

Strategies to become more optimistic:

- You can be optimistic without leaving reality.
- Change your inner monologue so that new patterns of thinking can be developed.

- Practice positive affirmations. I like this one from Joseph Murphy, "I am born to succeed; the infinite within me cannot fail." Incantations feeds the soul and brings out the best in you. Do what Joyce Myers said, "speak victory into your life."

- To every disappointment there is an added benefit. You have to believe that. Winners win because they don't allow misfortune, challenges, loss or setbacks derail their efforts or shortcut their expectations.

- Avoid people who don't support you or see the best in you. Avoid people who always try to bring up all the mistakes you've made and deliberately criticize you. Someone who means you well will uplift your spirit and encourage you along.

_____ Chapter 6 _____

RESULTS-ORIENTED

VICTO**R**Y

If you care enough about your results, you will almost certainly attain them.

– William James

Results are the outcome of expectations. The pursuit of a goal is often mobilized by one's desired result and what one hopes to gain by pursuing it. It's because of desired results that people sustain their persistence over long periods. It's imperative to have clearly specified goals that encompass the expectations to be achieved. When you are clear about what you want, the brain develops cognitive maps to help you zoom in on it. A mental image solidifies expectations in a way that helps to create know-hows for achievement.

The first Emperor of Rome was Julius Caesar's great nephew Augustus. Caesar had adopted him not long before his death. He is known as one of the greatest leaders of Rome. Augustus ruled for 49 years and seemed to have accomplished all that Caesar had hoped to achieve during his short reign. A dynasty was created that lasted for almost a century. It seems that even in death Caesar still accomplished what he originally wanted. The adoption of his nephew showed how result-oriented Caesar was. He wanted to create a dynasty that prolonged his legacy.

The uninitiated often thinks about the hurdles, obstacles, mistakes, and all the other negative junk of failure. Not realizing or realizing too late that focusing on the negatives is often the reason for their failure. Caesar still achieved his goals, even in death. Obviously, people stick with their goals because of the end results, not what they are going through at the moment. Result is what happens as a consequence of pursuing your goals. It is that which follows because of the effort or work you put in. So naturally, if you exert great efforts in attaining your goals your results might be different when compared to half-hearted efforts.

What is it that you hope to gain from the goal you have? What will it do for you? Will it help you to gain respect, influence, wealth, friends, what? Why is it important to you to remain vigilant towards attaining it? Before you take the first step towards pursuing anything, you must know your whys or reasons. In writing this book, I've come to realize that writing has always been my passion, and I've always immersed myself in it. Imagine writing something that could change the course of someone's life, help them to evaluate their skills and capabilities to know how to go about taking certain action.

What is the thinking behind the goal you have? Maybe you started a business. You obviously think it will give you something more, which is why you took the chance. There is nothing small about starting a business or wanting to be your own boss. But why was it important to you to do that? Will it increase your income? Are you imagining how people will react when they use your product or service? Will they be happy with it and want to tell all their friends? Maybe just thinking about your independence and the freedom you would have created for yourself is enough.

Why do you want to become a millionaire? What is the lifestyle you are imagining? Will it allow you to travel to many exotic destinations that you've always dreamed about? Perhaps being a millionaire will allow you to help the underprivileged, and you can make more of a difference in the world. Perhaps your goal is to get your Master's Degree because you know you will get an increased salary or a promotion. It might encourage you to find a better job someplace else. It would help make a great example in your family. Whatever the reason, it has to be good. The results you're after have to move the needle point somehow. It must be life altering. It must pull you forward. That's the reason why you have to set your goals really high, challenging and specific. Your goals have to be so big they scare you. It must stretch you. A goal must help you to grow; it must make you better than you are. It must ignite your passion. It must take you over yonder.

Bill Gates' vision was that he wanted a computer on every desk and in every home. Remember in the early days computers were not popular. Many must have thought him crazy. That was such a bold and ambitious vision. What is yours? What is your vision or philosophy for your life? Make it as big as possible. Les Brown said, "Shoot for the moon and even if you miss, you'll still land among stars."

- ✓ Charles Schwab's vision was, "helping investors help themselves."
- ✓ Walt Disney's was to, "make people happy."
- ✓ Ben and Jerry's vision was, "making the best possible ice cream, in the nicest possible way."
- ✓ Google's vision is, "to provide the world's information in one click."
- ✓ John F. Kennedy said, "I believe that this nation should commit itself to achieving the goal before this decade is out of landing a man on the moon and returning him home safely."

Key Lessons about Results from Caesar and Bill Gates:

- Caesar set his sights on conquering Rome. Results proved promising with each defeat of the tribes, each campaign brought him closer to the ultimate prize.

- One important lesson from Caesar was that he adopted his nephew so his dreams could still be realized after his death. Passing the baton to his nephew who would fully execute his goal was perhaps Caesar's best decision. Because after his assassination, Octavian (Augustus) ruled for 49 years and was labeled one of Rome's best leaders.

- When Bill Gates created that vision the Internet resembled a mystical province. It must have seemed crazy to many, especially if they were not in the world of computer technology. "Today's lunacy is tomorrow's conventional wisdom," said Jack Welch.

- It is obvious that results were important to Gates. Now that his first vision is fully realized, he is currently part of a global effort to reduce inequality. There is little doubt that he can achieve that too.

- In math, a result is the quantity or expression obtained by calculation. So it is with your goals. What do you calculate you will achieve at the end? How much money will it be? How many people will you have helped? How many lives changed?

Personal Result Moment:

Result-oriented motives influence many achievement situations. Although I wanted to run my own business and achieve great things with it, I never had any solid reasons why. My focus changed, however, when I created a vision as well as a mission for my business. My mission was to speak in every high school in New York. I have been in many since then. Of course I realized how crazy that must have been because New York City has an extremely high number of high schools in all five boroughs. My vision on the other hand is to become a worldwide leader in motivating, uplifting, and empowering everyday people. Whenever I call up a school to ask for a speaking opportunity, I always tell them about my mission. It's important to let people know what your intentions are.

People will never know your intentions by just looking at you. It has to be what you convey to them that will inform them of what you are about. Perhaps that's the reason why many companies have their mission or vision statements as you enter the building or office, so right off the bat you know what their values are and why they exist. When you convey your vision and mission you are in essence revealing the results you want to obtain.

It is also a great way to remind everyone about your direction. Missions, visions and values are forgotten sometimes which is why many lose focus. Many companies fail because they forgot why they started in the first place.

Why People fail to get results:

If you don't follow through how do you expect to get results? Many people give up not realizing that success was just around the corner. If they had stuck with it a while longer, they would have seen results. Confidence is important here because if you don't trust that you will achieve the results you want you might give up. When you calculate what you will achieve based on the efforts you put in, that should make you either feel good or feel bad. The only way you would feel bad is if you don't feel confident of a favorable outcome.

Strategies to Help Achieve Greater Results:

- You have to know and be clear about what it is you're after.
- Set your goals way above your own expectations. If that fails, shoot for higher still. It is when you stretch yourself that you see how far you can go.

- Write a vision statement. Be clear as to what your mission is. Having a daily/weekly mission can help check your progress. It is progress that makes people happy.

- Read several company visions/missions to get the gist of it. I mentioned a few in this chapter. Create one that's reflective of you.

- Staying focused is the key. Do not allow anyone to get in your head. People have told me that it is impossible to speak in every New York City High School. Believe me, I know that it seems far-fetched. Many schools say no to me. But when you set your goals high you probably get very near to your target. That's why it is important to have high standards. Keep your vision somewhere you can see it and read it regularly.

- When you broaden your vision you are giving your dreams a fighting chance.

_____ Chapter 7 _____

YEARNING

VICTOR**Y**

Some people dream of great accomplishments,

while others stay awake and do them

– Anonymous

You will not pursue something that you have no desire for. Without a yearning desire nothing is ever achieved. Desire is an instigator, it provokes action and it is what sets the pace. Desire wields with an intent to act and often anchors intention. Desire first, intention second, but both are influenced by personal motivation. Desire is similar to a craving, a wish, a hunger, or an urge. If you are hungrier to win, chances are you will be the winner, but taken all the qualities mentioned in this book into consideration. Studies have shown that desires affect decision making and goal-directed behavior. Some would argue that when individuals are expressing their intention they are in fact expressing their desires. When individuals express their intentions to act, they are revealing as well a level of self-confidence pertinent to the act they intend to perform. One's expectations of the future are often embroiled in a desire to achieve the things wished for. Nowhere is the evidence more pronounced of the actual outcome of things desired than in the lives and accomplishments of the historical characters mentioned in this book. All intentions have a desired outcome which is meant to satisfy a need, want, goal, ambition, or activity.

Margaret Thatcher must have had a yearning desire for political power, success, or simply making a difference, which is why she succeeded in vehemently ruling Great Britain for three consecutive terms. Before Meryl Streep played her in Iron Lady, I thought about her and wondered whether she was still alive. Jamaica, where I grew up, was greatly influenced by the British, and in fact, was under British control from 1655 – 1962. After slavery was abolished in 1834, Jamaica quickly began working on gaining independence, which was only achieved in 1962. I remember reading about Thatcher when I was growing up and admired her strength as a woman and political leader. It is fair to say that without desire Thatcher wouldn't have made it to the height of political power that she did. Remember, desire is what is transmuted into power. Without the desire she wouldn't have had the urge to make things better. Without desire nothing is pursued. Her first two attempts at political life ended in defeat. She ran for a candidate seat in Parliament. Soon after her defeat she got married, had twins Carol and Mark and went back to school to study law.

She returned in winning form however, when in 1959 she finally won a seat in the House of Commons. Thatcher quickly moved up in rank, first she was appointed Education Minister, and then conservative leader, leader of the opposition followed, then the highest rank of all Prime Ministers of Great Britain in 1979. She held on to political power with an iron-like grip for so long that, even after she left office, her radicalism was still felt. No one can deny even after 30 years her influence in Great Britain, and indeed the world. You have to remember also that this was a woman. If a man were that tough and forceful no one would think it odd, but a woman having those qualities made her a standout. She once said that,

"It may be the cock that crows, but it is the hen that lays the eggs."

It's evident in people who have achieved great power or wealth that they started with a desire. Looking at your life and what you want to achieve, are you passionate about it? Do you go to bed thinking about ways and means to make it happen? When you wake up, are you riveted to continue your journey? What is it about your goal that fills you with excitement? If you want it so badly that you can taste it, then that's the driving force you need.

No doubt Thatcher's task was tremendous. She had to have had an agenda and she held on to power long enough so most of it could be realized. When she took office the country was entering a recession, unemployment doubled, the manufacturing industry closed down due to its inefficiency, interest rates had to be raised to control inflation, and indirect taxes had to be increased. Tough measures had to be implemented to fix those ills.

The Falklands War was another debacle. Argentina invaded the Falklands and that created added pressure on an already fragile Britain. The Falklands had long been vulnerable, and since talks at the United Nations had collapsed, it left a gap wide open to revive a plan that had been inactive for a while. Argentina was claiming that it was unjust the way Great Britain had control over the islands. Although Britain had control since 1833, Argentina was of the assumption that they had inherited rights to the islands. So on April 2nd they invaded hoping to get what they thought was rightfully theirs.

Britain, seemingly undeterred, set sail a task force of 100 ships and by May 2nd 320 men of just one Argentine cruiser were dead. Overall 650 Argentines were killed. Argentina surrendered on June 14th, 1982. It is fair to say that the defeatist mood in Britain could have overshadowed the success of the combat in the islands. The invasion occurred shortly after Thatcher first won the Prime Minister's seat. Words such as humiliation and resignation were being thrown around. It was perhaps the success of the war of the Falkland Islands why Thatcher was re-elected for her second term.

During this same time, trade dominance was prevalent. The strikes created many blackouts leaving many without light. Things were so bad Britain came close to becoming a Third World state. According to Mail Online, "the 34 years between the defeat of Hitler in 1945 and the conservative party victory in 1979 general election was an era of failure and humiliation."

Yet by the end of her reign in 1990 she'd managed to reshape and revive Britain's economy and politics, forged successful relationships with other world leaders, improved people's psychology of decline, and reinvigorated foreign policy. There was no question that she did a great job. Maybe her radicalism was an advantage, but it seemed to have been a disadvantage, too. The opposition desperately wanted her out and after eleven years in power they finally succeeded.

Key Lessons Learned from Margaret Thatcher:

- Be uncompromising in your efforts to achieve what you want by knowing that what you want is not up for debate.
- The bigger picture, which is your end result means more than any disagreement you might have with people who don't have the same vision. Although Thatcher was doing well and results started

showing, there were many who were against the way she conducted business.

- It is more significant to be result-oriented than to be combative. When people started seeing results of her leadership, they voted again to keep her at the top. Her agenda was to get Britain back on its feet, which is a clear indication of her mission and values.

- Thatcher was so tough, no one could easily push her off the road.

- It you look at the conditions of Great Britain's economy back then, it is indicative to treachery, obstacles, negative circumstances, setbacks, criticisms, and defeat, all excuses used by people who don't succeed. But it is apparent that Thatcher was inspired to do something about it rather than be defeated by it.

Where does Desire come from?

Desire is a craving that logic cannot repress. It's a hunger that developed out of an element that resonated with an individual. The thing desired becomes self-defining to the point where it becomes part of their identity. If you have no desires there won't be any passion to fuel victory. Because desire is so widespread over a great cross-section of human needs it affects our need to be proficient, accomplished, and valued. Thatcher had passion, and no doubt that was what drove her politically. You won't succeed without the desire or the intention to succeed. Desire is emotion-based and runs parallel to passion in this book. Passion and desire is something that can burn your insides, because the activity you like is highly valued. It appeared that all the historical figures mentioned in this book burned inside because they were so passionate about what they wanted. Their desire was their fuel. They failed so many times but kept trying and trying until they succeeded.

Failure has the tendency of reducing one's desires and I imagine that's the problem why many don't continue to pursue their dreams. But success is about never giving up, remember? You simply get back on track by remembering your achievement outcomes. Failure can fuel persistence, in a sense where many redirect or re-engineer their paths, fortifying a new sense of direction.

- **How to Increase Your Desires:**

- Your goal must have a why. Why is it important to you? Why does your goal resonate? Why do you like what you're pursuing? Your "whys" give you the power to act effectively. Your "whys" are what power you forward. You have to have a why to start. Remember the condition Britain was in at the time? There was enough "why" for Margaret Thatcher that she said, "I can't bear to see Britain's decline, I just can't."

- What you want must be meaningful with more than just a momentary pass. Thatcher approached the Prime Minister and told him she was going to make a try for the seat. He never spoke to her again. She saw that the country was not getting better, she thought she could make a difference, and make a difference she did.

- Desire intensifies the feeling of want so immensely that it literally pulls you forward.

_____Chapter 8_____

MASTERING YOUR BLUEPRINT

The only way of finding the limits of the possible is to go

beyond them into the impossible

– Author Clarke

In Robert Kiyosaki's video "60 Minutes to Getting Rich" he said that his natural inclination is to be poor, but he had to fight against that to be rich. I think many of us can relate to that. It seems because most of us weren't taught how to be rich we spend most of our lives wondering if it is at all possible. If we were taught this subject in school I believe most of us would have acquired the mental faculty that would increase the likelihood of the success ideation.

Since there is empirical evidence to show that a person can condition his or her mind to achieve great things, the traits previously discussed can be cultivated or mastered. When you condition your mind using incantations, being more optimistic about your results, or being proactive in your endeavors, you are in essence mastering your blueprint.

Psychology and Behavior

Conditioning of the mind is a common theme in psychology. In fact, it was some of the earliest psychologists who initiated the behaviorism theory that brought conditioning to the forefront. It is basically a form of learning that results in a shift in behavior or helps to reshape one's behavior. That's why practice makes perfect or at least makes improvements.

Since psychology is the study of human behavior it makes sense to mention this subject briefly. The father of behaviorism John B. Watson thought that behavior can be measured, trained and changed. Environmental stimuli can also shape behavior. With that said, when you practice riding a bike, for example, it becomes easier to do. When you reinforce behavior the behavior is strengthened.

When you see tiny progress based on your efforts it encourages or increases a positive response.

Psychology is important to your blueprint. In fact it affects everything. When individuals are deficient in certain mental faculties they also lack the ability to stick with a goal. Hence, developing these faculties increases your chances of achieving and succeeding. Your mental faculties have a whole lot to do with your conscious and subconscious mind. In the book "Power of the Subconscious Mind" by Dr. Joseph Murphy, he teaches how to unlock the powers of the subconscious. He said that you can achieve whatever you want based on what you feed your mind. Whatever the mind is consistently fed develops into a pattern that inevitably changes one's behavior and outcome.

If you have not been able to achieve any level of success, you have to realize at this moment that conditioning your mindset is 80% of the process in achieving what you want. What are you telling yourself on a daily basis? What is the script of your inner dialogue? Perhaps you need to rewrite it. If you can make it your daily mission to improve some aspect of your life particularly the way you are thinking, half the battle is already won.

Your subconscious mind feeds from your habit, the pattern you created. Imagine therefore living with a negative outlook consistently. That's why a reinforced behavior is strengthened or increased, it changes behavior positively. Also, that's why you learn how to do things after you've practiced several times because it's transferred to your long term memory. Habitually doing and thinking the same thing is the habit of the subconscious. These habitual thoughts whether positive or negative become your life. The subconscious mind is very powerful and is one of the mental faculties that can create your success or dish the negative ruins of your thinking.

Obviously, victory is not simply about thinking positively, what gives you power is the amount of action you decide to take. It influences motivation and effort as well as one's goal-directed activities. No doubt you would have realized by now the importance of self-motivation, self-confidence, and how to monitor yourself in terms of the goals you intend to pursue. Conditioning affects behavior, so you will be more inclined to start doing something towards the goal you are imagining.

Your Blueprint

"The goals you set for yourself and the strategies you choose becomes your blueprint or plan," said Charles Given. Your personal blueprint must be rock solid or definite for it to be effective. When you are building a house setting a strong foundation is paramount to the structure. The same can be said about your goals. What are the steps that will take you to victory? How do you plan on getting to where you want to be? Here are a few ideas that can help you.

- You have to know exactly what you want, so make it clear. There should be no doubt that you want to be a nurse, an illustrator, a professional athlete, a teacher, a writer. Self-regulation, and how you monitor your steps in the process of achievement are important elements.
- Make a list of everything you can do to achieve what you want. Just having your goals in your mind is not enough. Somehow, when you write things

down, that act alone serves to crystalize the information in your mind and it becomes real.

- Set weekly/monthly goals. Short-term goals increases the effectiveness of your plans. Tiny progress makes a huge difference to any long term endeavor.

- There are short-term and long-term goals. According to your list you should know which falls under what category. Obviously some goals take a while longer to manifest. Short-term goals works like enthusiastic supporter of your long-term goals.

- Your plan should show the different stages of your achievements.

- I learned several years ago that successful people have written goals. It's important to write things down, a busy lifestyle tending to work and family can cause you to lose focus or dim the light of the goals you want.

Life Changing Quotations

While I was living in Jamaica I started compiling a list of quotes. I made a booklet from typing sheets by cutting each sheet into four pieces and stapling the edges together. I since have journals. Whenever I find new quotes I would write them in this booklet. I would read them every day. It seemed to have transformed me unconsciously because looking back I was really gutsy and never understood why. The quotes inspired me and made me confident, bold, and fearless. I was pushing boundaries although I didn't realize it then.

Jamaica is a beautiful place to live and an even better place for a vacation, but the economic climate can be harsh. Still, that was not the reason why I was one of the few who had three great jobs. I felt like I could achieve great things, and I wasn't afraid to try. I traveled with my booklet to the United States when I emigrated here in 2001. It was much later that I realized the power of those words. My booklet got lost over the years, but I am still in the habit of writing quotes down in my journal.

There are a few incantations at the back of this book or perhaps you already have some of your own. Whatever the case, use them to empower yourself.

Final Points to Remember:

- Nobody can change your mindset for you; this is something you're going have to work on for yourself. It's tough changing after you've been in a fixed state of mind all your life. But I learned that when you change, it ultimately extends something within you.

- Perhaps success is elusive because it feels like a foreign concept to you. If the last fifteen, ten or five years look very familiar with no improvement, no growth, no change, then it's time for a mindset change. Mix things up a bit. "Devote today to do something so daring, not even you can believe you're doing it," said Oprah Winfrey.

- You have to demand what you want from yourself. You are the one in control. You're in the driver's seat. Whatever you put into your mind, your plans, and ambitions, that's in your control. If achieving your goals is forcing you to walk an extra mile, so what? You should be loyal to your pursuits.

- Conditioning your mind is also about changing your belief system. Can you realistically see yourself as a successful person? In your mind's eye you should be advancing, progressing, and moving forward. If these things are difficult for you to visualize or imagine, try repeating these incantations while staring at yourself in the mirror. Not just once, but daily.

- It's time you start feeding your mind a new script. You were born to have a fulfilling abundant life.

- Before constructing a building or a house it is necessary to see the architectural plan and its drawings. The goals you are working on and the strategies that you plan to use to achieve them are your blueprint. Mastering your blueprint, therefore, is mastering the strategies that will allow you to better achieve the goals you're presently pursuing.

- According to the book *Power of the Subconscious Mind*, "habit is the function of the subconscious." When you learn something based on repetition, that's your subconscious mind at work.

_____ *Chapter 9* _____

HOW TO TURN DEFEAT INTO VICTORY

Victory is sweetest when you've known defeat

-Malcolm Forbes

Resilience is a powerful process of rebounding and reintegration. Overcoming the trials of misfortune, depression, illness, uncertainty or change is challenging even to those who consider themselves tough. The potential vulnerabilities created by these events leave many in despair, incapacitated and with an unwillingness to cope. Thankfully, resilience can be cultivated along any stage of a lifespan. There are protective factors or defense mechanisms that can be accessed internally or from one's social environment, but outcomes are often different for each individual. Tell-tale sign as to why some remain defeated while others persevere. Environmental risks found in adversity threaten victory on different levels for different people. Outcomes are never the same, although some might have gone through the same experience, an indication of the importance of retaining a positive psychological outlook during adverse situations. A defeatist mentality leads to maladaptive outcomes.

A relationship exists between coping skills, adaptability and self-efficacy in overcoming threats, illness, stress, disaster, tragedy, difficulty or hardship. For resilience to be an effective process these components work together as a protective alliance for turning adversity into victory. Developing these qualities means a person can effectively overcome any trial or tribulation that comes their way. This mechanism characterizes the competence one must possess for power over adversity.

Coping Skills

It is obvious that some people have better coping skills. These coping skills are intimately linked to their protective alliances. Coping is a strategy used to offset threats, disadvantages and change. Coping is subsumed under one's personality, which is why some are able to cope and adapt more effectively than others.

Subsequently, the kind of strategy an individual enacts to overcome adversity is closely tied to the type of personality he or she possesses and the adaptive or maladaptive outcome he or she achieves. Coping skills during environmentally challenging situations strengthen one's resiliency and improve competence. How people cope with adversity is a testament to their psychological well-being, inherent within an individual. Defeat comes from either the internal or external demands in one's environment that have proven to exceed all the stratagems people think they possess. A person's protective alliances therefore often annihilate these patterns of defeatist thinking by creating, reframing, reintegrating or reinvigorating coping mechanisms that reinstall a sense of purpose, so as to regain some semblance of normalcy. Coping, therefore, is a form of resilience that manages adversity in some way, shape or form.

Adaptability

There is an adaptability factor evident in people who have overcome defeat. Central to coping is adaptation and the capacity to evolve from adversity to a better state.

Change, unexpected or not, positive or negative, requires flexibility to adjust to altering states/environments. Throughout anyone's lifespan, change occurs on a number of occasions: a marriage or relationship ended, change from high school to college, from college to a work environment, from one job to the next, from being single to being married, from having no kids to having a two or three or from being healthy to being ill. To many, these are combustible changes. To be adaptable to these changing situations and conditions requires an ability to acclimatize oneself using a protective alliance of self-efficacy, self-determinism and one's interpersonal relationships. These can be used constructively through self-regulation. Often, it is the change from routine to being outside of one's comfort zone and the inability to handle that transition that leads to defeat. Getting habituated to a new environment unsettles many but it offers a great advantage.

The question as to how one adapts to an environment that is always unpredictable is answered in the items below:

· Learn quickly how to do things differently.

·   Reorganize, restructure and adjust plans or strategies that did not work the first time instead of accepting defeat.

·   Adaptation is a process of reintegration that requires a buoyant disposition.

·   Making light of the adaptation process instead of stressing over it increases the likelihood of a successful transition and the capabilities one needs to cope with adversity.

Self-efficacy

The personal resource in one's protective alliance offers a positive assimilation to the uncertainty that change presents.   Negotiating mentally to what is new or uncertain requires adjustment, and this is where self-efficacy comes into play. First of all, it is clear that some changes are extremely difficult, severe, critical, even life-changing, and getting by might simply not be enough. But self-efficacy is a defense mechanism guided by one's belief in one's capacity to overcome and remain vigilant through hard times. With self-efficacy greater effort is utilized. There is a greater need to hammer on, to persist and go the distance. Rutter (1990) said that "resilience arises out of a belief in one's own self-efficacy, the ability to deal with change and a use of a repertoire of social problem-solving skills." In any goal attainment setting, adversity is ever present, but a person's perceived self-efficacy, if it is strong enough, provides a defense that can tackle the most arduous of situations and circumstances.

The personality traits from chapters 1 – 7 form a framework from which coping skills, adaptability and self-efficacy can be built, ultimately forging a positive negotiating tool for rebounding. It is from the utilization of these tools that many are able to override potential vulnerabilities. They can be mastered and cultivated daily to facilitate the conquest of any goal, overturn failures or misfortune and build a solid core that can serve any individual throughout his or her lifespan.

_____*Chapter 10*_____

GAUGE YOUR TRAITS

----

*You cannot dream yourself into a character you must
hammer and forge yourself one*

James A. Froude

In gauging your traits, you evaluate your skillset and capabilities to know how to go about taking certain action. In any self-assessment, information is revealed about what each person holds true about themselves which is often manifested over a broad cross section of their lives. Traits are steady elements, so if one is confident at work, he/she should be confident at a party, a game, in school, in large groups, as well as small groups. How you value yourself shouldn't change with the environment. The magnitude of these traits, therefore, are felt and utilized in every walk of life. With the stability of optimism for example, it's often maintained even when setbacks or challenges present themselves. The traits presented here are positively related to an emotional stability which doesn't fluctuate during turbulent times, and is likely as a consequence to help individuals achieve their goals.

Be Honest in your assessment.

V.I.C.T.O.R.Y MODEL			
Classifications	Solid (Unyielding)	Half-way (Easily discouraged)	Weak (Susceptible to defeat)
Vivacious/Enthusiastic			
Initiative/proactive			
Confidence			
Tenacity			
Optimism			
Result-oriented			
Yearning/desire			

Strength: *In this category, individuals have a positive perspective, knows who they are and is unyielding in their beliefs, convictions and decisions.*
Half-way: *Being half-way is being somewhat vulnerable in many situations since the individual is not entirely committed.*
Weak: *Wishy washy and ineffectual pattern. Always uncertain in decision making and lacking guts to take action.*

Use your results to improve any shortcomings, take necessary action, increase your self-understanding, engage in self-evaluation and improve the properties that enhances goal-directed activities. Keep your results in mind when doing a presentation, hosting an event or socializing in general. Gauge yourself to be at your best wherever you are. Add a little enthusiasm if it's lacking, develop some gumption and be proactive, increase your desires by realizing what resonates with you. Below average confidence or tenacity will not shift the needle point. Spice up your personality daily by adding a combination of these characteristics. This will eventually become you. This is how you cultivate and master the principles that drive you from one level to the next. This is how you grow.

_____CONCLUSION_____

I am happy you have finished reading this book. At this juncture you should have developed some drive, motivation, and an "I can do this" attitude. I hope you realize that the concept is all about who you need to become to achieve the goals you want. To achieve victory requires calculated discipline, comprehensive tactical intention, and attention of laser-like focus. Each chapter gave examples of some of the most legendary figures of history. You will agree that they were trailblazers rich in ideas and chutzpah. Did you jot down any ideas? What was your favorite chapter? I would love to know what you thought was interesting and thought-provoking that you highlighted or underlined it. You should read those points daily and keep it as reminders. The tools described are for guidance. It is a recipe for success, after all. Every recipe has a method and you cannot achieve great success without the right methods or overarching strategy.

The bigger the goal the more these characteristics are necessary. Goals are supposed to be challenging. Goals need motivation as a function to help satisfy a need to be successful. Self-confidence requires self-esteem as both depend on each other to strive for and accomplish goals. This is one of the major reasons why most goals are not met or people simply refuse to set lofty goals because they don't have these qualities in them. Research shows that goals are not realized when these are missing. Striving to achieve a goal that has proven to be difficult requires a belief system that has all these elements attached, because they are all connected.

The trailblazers mentioned in the chapters were so committed to their dreams and passionate in their endeavors that success was inevitable. There are a lot of lessons in Martin Luther King's dream, for example. It seemed impossible or too ambitious at the time, didn't it? His dream is still kicking butts and taking names!

Big Goals of History:

The following are some of the biggest goals in history that seemed near impossible to achieve at the time. The bottom line is, if you don't have the qualities mentioned in this book, any goal, no matter how petty, will appear impossible.

Abraham Lincoln: His dream was to end slavery. The Emancipation Proclamation was born. The final enactment came after his assassination.

Thomas Edison: Dreamed of a lamp that could function with electricity. This was not realized until more than 6,000 failed attempts.

Henry Ford: Buying a car in the early 1900s was a big expense many could not afford. Ford's goal was to make affordable, simple and reliable cars that average Americans could easily afford.

Napoleon Hill: Was asked by Andrew Carnegie to write a book on the philosophy of achievement. His book *Think and Grow Rich* has become a motivational classic.

Martin Luther King, Jr.: "I have a dream that one day this nation will rise up and live out the true meaning of its creed: 'We hold these truths to be self-evident, that all men are created equal'."

Harriet Tubman: "Children, if you are tired, keep going; if you are scared keep going; if you are hungry keep going; if you want to taste freedom, keep going." Guiding slaves to freedom was Tubman's goal and vision. She freed more than 300 slaves.

There are so many other goals and historical figures I could have mentioned but people today are also doing extraordinary things. Technological advancement and strides in health care/treatment represent many goals that have been realized. The Internet according to Bill Clinton was "like a mystical province" some years ago. Now it is the fabric of our lives.

_____The End_____

_____Recommended Books_____

Break from the Pack - Oren Harari

The Think Big Manifesto - Michael Port

Book Yourself Solid - Michael Port

Winning - Jack Welch

Trump 101, The way to Success - Donald Trump

Think Big and Kick Ass - Donald Trump

What makes the Great Great - Dennis Kimbro

Think and Grow Rich - Napoleon Hill

The 48 Laws of Power - Robert Greene

The Miracle of Mind Dynamics - Joseph Murphy

The Power of the Subconscious mind - Joseph Murphy

Think Yourself Rich - Joseph Murphy

Decide and Conquer - Stephen Robbins

Awakening the Entrepreneur within - Michael Gerber

WITHDRAWN

Made in the USA
Middletown, DE
14 September 2016